For K.L.   K.E.

Text by Elena Pasquali
Illustrations copyright © 2010 Lucia Mongioj
This edition copyright © 2010 Lion Hudson

The moral rights of the author and illustrator
have been asserted

A Lion Children's Book
an imprint of
Lion Hudson plc
Wilkinson House, Jordan Hill Road,
Oxford OX2 8DR, England
www.lionhudson.com
ISBN 978 0 7459 6210 8

First edition 2010
1 3 5 7 9 10 8 6 4 2 0

A catalogue record for this book is available
from the British Library

Typeset in 20/25 Caslon Old Face BT
Printed in China July 2010 (manufacturer LH06)

Distributed by:
UK: Marston Book Services Ltd, PO Box 269, Abingdon, Oxon OX14 4YN
USA: Trafalgar Square Publishing, 814 N Franklin Street, Chicago, IL 60610
USA Christian Market: Kregel Publications, PO Box 2607, Grand Rapids, MI 49501

The Tale of Baboushka

Elena Pasquali

Illustrated by Lucia Mongioj

LION
CHILDREN'S

Baboushka's house was always spick and span.
For Baboushka loved to sweep and scrub,
to dust and polish
and make everything just so.

And Baboushka's things were neat and tidy.
For Baboushka loved to save and store,
to stitch and sew
and fill her cupboard with lovely things so nimbly made.

One wintry afternoon, as Baboushka was in her kitchen
peeling and chopping,
mixing and stirring,
there came a knock
at the door.

"What a bother," she said,
as she wiped her hands.
"And me in the middle of all this cooking."

When she opened the door —
well, what a surprise.

There were three tall travellers
bowing low,
their rich clothes glinting
in the setting sun.

"Might you have room," they humbly asked,
"for us to stay this snowy night?"
"For night is near."
"And we've travelled far."

"Of course, come in," Baboushka said.

And she tucked their boots by the chuckling fire
and hung their hats
and brushed their cloaks.

She brought them bread and soup and cheese
and cakes and figs and home-brewed ale.

"But what's in here?" Baboushka asked,
as she lifted their bags
to the attic door.

"Gifts for a king," the travellers whispered.
"A king for whom a new star shines –
the king of love, the prince of peace."

That night, while all the house was sleeping,
the snow clouds cleared and that same bright star shone.

First the cat, and then Baboushka,
looked up to see its golden light.

"Look! That's the star," she told the cat,
she told the dog,
she told the mouse.

"The light that shines for the king of love.
The light that shines for the prince of peace."

And at once she wanted to give her gift:
a gift from the heart,
a gift of her hands,
a gift of love.

The next day came, and soon the travellers
were ready to set out on their way.

"I have gifts," said kind Baboushka,
"for you to take to the king of love."

"You must come!" they said, "Come now, with us.
Leave cares aside and follow the king."

"Oh… no!" said Baboushka. "I… I'm not quite ready…
I'll find your footsteps, and I'll watch for the star."

"But first I must sweep and clean and tidy

and wash and iron

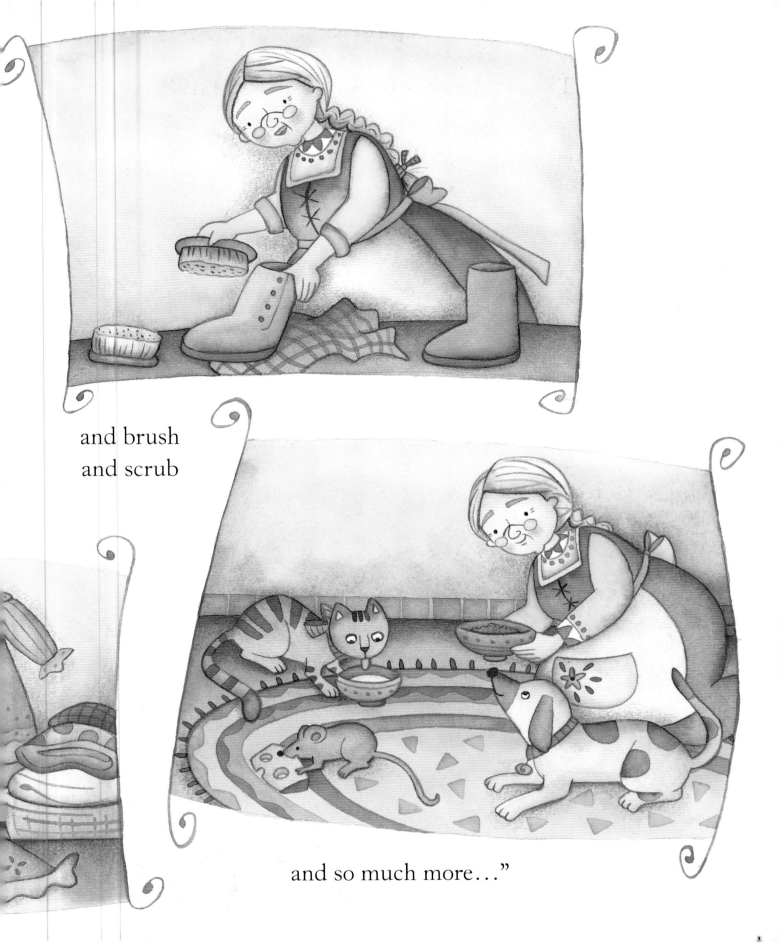

and brush
and scrub

and so much more…"

As Baboushka worked, the hours ticked by:
a snow-swept day and a frosty night.

When she set out, she could find no footsteps.
In the darkening sky were the same old stars.

"Oh dear," she said. "But I have my gifts…
and I do so want to see this king."

Baboushka set out without guide or starlight
to find the child who was born to be king.

But on the way she saw so many children
who would be so pleased by a lovely gift.

So she left a gift here

and here

and here

and here.

Still she is seeking.
Still she is giving,
and all for the sake
of the king of love.

Other titles from Lion Children's Books

Ituku's Christmas Journey   *Elena Pasquali & Dubravka Kolanovic*

Papa Panov's Special Day   *Mig Holder & Julie Downing*

The Fourth Wise Man   *Mary Joslin & Richard Johnson*